DIRTY
LITTLE
COLLEGE
SECRETS

DIRTY LITTLE COLLEGE SECRETS

Getting In, Staying In, and Graduating

Lisa Ann Zanglin EdD

gatekeeper press™

Tampa, Florida

Dirty Little College Secrets
Getting In, Staying In, and Graduating

Published by Gatekeeper Press
7853 Gunn Hwy, Suite 209
Tampa, FL 33626
www.GatekeeperPress.com

This publication is designed to provide accurate and authoritative information in regard to the subject matter covered. It is sold with the understanding that the publisher is not engaged in rendering legal or accounting services. If legal advice or other expert assistance is required, the services of a competent professional person should be sought.

ISBN (Paperback): 9781662955945
ISBN (eBook): 9781662955952

PREFACE

I've spent over twenty years in higher education. I've developed undergraduate and graduate programs, sat on curriculum, accreditation, and scholarship committees, and taught countless hours in the classroom. I've been an advisor to thousands of students, and I'm still surprised by how many administrative and faculty mistakes prevent a student from graduating. Hopefully, this book will prevent some of those mistakes.

This book combines real-life experience and over two decades of expertise, talking to numerous parents and students in the turmoil of the college admissions process and during college. The purpose of this book is to help students and parents answer some basic questions about the college admittance process, requirements, scholarships, grades, class selection, and other topics that may help a student graduate. It's not a book on how to "beat the system" or tell the readers how to cheat, but there are existing loopholes that may enhance academic results and provide debt-free financing for college. Don't blame the people using them. The organizations should change the rules to close the loopholes.

I've attended two college orientations for my children and participated in hundreds of orientations as a professor.

While they are useful, there was still a great deal of information they didn't share. Parents and students find out the hard way, after it's too late to correct the problem. If you're a parent who didn't attend college, navigating the waters of higher education is even more difficult. The best advice I can give any future college student and their parents is this: **You are your own best advisor. Do your research.**

TABLE OF CONTENTS

CHAPTER 1

APPLYING TO COLLEGE

If you have a student in high school, they should have already begun their search, selected their top five choices, compiled what they need to be accepted, and ascertained the chances of being admitted to the college of choice. **DO NOT TRUST THE HIGH SCHOOL ADVISOR!** Like anything, there are good advisors, bad advisors, and lazy advisors. Most provide a decent overview of local colleges, in-state institutions, and general guidance on college acceptance requirements. Still, it is your responsibility to ensure you submit the correct paperwork, transcripts, fees, and other required information to the colleges and, most importantly, *meet the deadlines.*

Many colleges have *early acceptance policies*, which begin at the end of your junior year in high school. Ensure you or your student start the process early and begin taking standardized tests during sophomore year in high school. Failure to meet deadlines is still the responsibility of the student applying to the college, but high schools have responsibilities to parents and students. If the high school counselor doesn't meet their obligations, however, the student ultimately pays the price for their incompetence.

Test, test, and retest. Although the ACT (American College Testing) seems easier than the SAT (Scholastic Aptitude Test), I recommend taking both standardized tests. The writing portion of the ACT is optional at this time, so most colleges do not require it, but it is good practice. There are also pretest versions of both of these tests, and it is a good idea to take them in eighth grade or sooner so the student is familiar with the format and becomes comfortable taking the exam.

I also recommend students take the Armed Services Vocational Aptitude Battery (ASVAB). Military recruiters give this exam to measure a student's skills and strengths in traditional subjects like English, Math, and Science, as well as proficiency in mechanics, computers, and electronics. The military uses the test to measure an applicant's aptitude in a given area and gives the student a score in each area. This can assist in focusing the student toward a given area of study. A score of 50 is average, and different services have minimum acceptance scores. If a student wants to become a helicopter mechanic in the Air Force, they may need a minimum score of 65 in the mechanical portion and a composite score of 60 on the overall exam. The minimum score change may depend on the needs of the military. Armed Forces recruiters and service websites can provide the various scores for each specialty in the military. Even if a student has no interest in joining the military, the ASVAB is a good exam to practice before the ACT/SAT.

Standardized tests are constantly updated, but most follow the same format for various subjects/categories, with a set number of questions and a time limit for each section.

One thing to remember when you take any standardized test is that they are usually multiple-choice, and you do not need to know the correct answer. If you can identify the wrong answers, you can significantly increase your chance of picking the correct response. For example, if there are four answers and you know two are incorrect, you have a 50/50 chance of choosing the right answer, even if you don't know it. There are volumes published on how to take a standardized test. Here is my best advice based on experience and research:

1. Practice taking the test numerous times.
2. Eliminate the wrong answers if you don't know the correct answer.
3. Your first guess is usually correct.
4. Watch the time and don't panic. If the test grades on all questions attempted and you don't think you'll finish, leave a couple of minutes and fill in the remaining answers. You are likely to get a couple correct.
5. Drink water, coffee, or other beverages to stay awake and focused.
6. Don't stress about your score. It's not the end of the world if you don't do well. Later in the book, I'll explain Super Scoring on the ACT, which can improve your overall composite score.
7. Retake the exam if you don't like your score.

TRUE STORY: A Catholic school in Alabama, had a school counselor who did not send in the transcripts of the valedictorian to Auburn University on time for the student to meet the admission and scholarship requirements. Auburn University was the student's first choice, and he was offered a full four-year tuition scholarship. The valedictorian had a

4.0 GPA, a 32 ACT, and could have had scholarships at other universities. He declined other offers because he was offered a scholarship at his college of choice. Auburn University required the transcripts to be sent directly from the school counselor. The school counselor assured the student that all documentation was sent to Auburn University. In October, the only required document was updated transcripts, which the school counselor neglected to send because most schools in the area required the transcripts to be sent in November. The counselor missed the deadline, and when Auburn did not receive the final documentation, the scholarship was rescinded. The counselor did not do his job, and the student did not take responsibility for his future. As a result, the valedictorian did not get into his school of choice, and because the acceptance date from other school scholarships had passed, he had no other scholarships and had to take out his loans to pay for another college. What happened to the school counselor? Nothing. The counselor apologized, but he was not fired from his position. Later that year, a friend offered the counselor a federal job, and he is now verifying requirements for an Associate's Degree education program for the Air Force. In essence, he received a promotion with a pay raise.

This example may be the exception, but it does happen, and since most scholarships are offered to incoming freshmen based on specific timelines, the best chance at a "free ride" or subsidized tuition to college is to meet all deadlines, apply early, and continue to communicate with the university on requirements to maintain the scholarship. Also, not all scholarships are published on a website. Call the university's scholarship department or the Dean or Department Head/Program Manager directly. Most departments have discretionary money they could award for scholarships, work-study, or women pursuing Science, Technology, Engineering, and Math (STEM) degrees. A friend's daughter majored in engineering to get a four-year scholarship and later majored in English, which she originally wanted to study. There are scholarships for almost everything but finding them is a challenge. Paying for college is a moot point unless you are accepted to college, so college acceptance should still be the primary focus.

I have sat on admittance boards, and most have a minimum set of criteria for acceptance. If you do not meet these standards, your packet will be at the bottom of the pile and will move up if the class quotas are not filled out. Different universities have different quotas based on a myriad of factors. The best way to ascertain these factors is to look at the incoming freshmen class demographics, grade point average, locations, income, etc. You may have to do some research, but these statistics are usually listed somewhere on the college websites and in their accreditation files. Once you know what the college is seeking, see where you fit into the acceptance standards and demographics, and you can gauge your chance of getting accepted to that specific university. However, there are also intangibles to consider, like sports, alumni, and boosters. Sometimes, it really is a matter of who you know and not what you know.

How can you increase your chance of acceptance? Obviously, scoring well on the ACT/SAT, high grades, and joining the right student organizations are necessary, but what else can you do to increase your chances of acceptance?

Diversity, inclusion, and equity have become popular in recent years, and most universities, especially Ivy League, are looking for ways to increase various demographics. I always tell parents to take a DNA test from one of the various testing kits on the market to check their race. The only race that requires verification documentation is Native American. If your DNA highlights the African continent, Mexico, or another area of the world that falls into a minority demographic, your student can check that box on demographics.

TRUE STORY: A non-minority, upper-middle-class family with well-educated parents knew it was an uphill battle for their son to be accepted to an Ivy League school. Their child had excellent grades from a competitive private school, the right clubs, played varsity sports, was very active in philanthropy, and planned to major in engineering. However, other white male students from the same area were not accepted to this university despite having higher grades in advanced placement courses and higher ACT/SAT scores than the minority students who received the scholarships and acceptance. The mother did a DNA test and found some very interesting results. Part of her heritage was from Africa. When the mother called her parents to inquire about their family tree and heritage, neither set of parents could confirm which relatives had originated from Africa. They were always told they were from Sicily and Greece. The father also did the "DNA and Me" test and was always told he was German and French. He was surprised to find a large circle over the Iberian Peninsula, which includes present day Spain. The mother had always thought she was Greek and Italian, but now she found out some of her relatives were from Africa and the father was of Spanish origins, her children could claim African-American and Spanish descent. The parents changed their son's race on his application, and the young man was admitted to the Ivy League school with a full scholarship.

This doesn't mean the young man would not have gained admittance regardless and obtained a full scholarship; however, in the past, the scholarship was not awarded to males who claimed "Caucasian" as their demographic.

Another demographic not discussed but widely used to accept students is *"first-generation college,"* which refers to, as one would assume, any student with parents who did not graduate from college. The Free Application for Student Financial Aid (FASFA) asks about "first-generation college students" when awarding grants and other financial aid, which will be discussed in a later chapter. This differs from "attended college" or graduated from a technical school. While this was the norm before 1950, it is much less common but an excellent way to get a grant, financial aid, or a scholarship to attend college. Grants do not have to be paid back, while loans currently must be paid back to the lending institution or the federal government, depending on where the loan originated. While none of this may seem fair, it is another consideration universities use to admit and pay tuition for future students.

CHAPTER 2

NOT ALL ACADEMIC GRADES FROM HIGH SCHOOL ARE CONSIDERED EQUAL

Grades matter, but it depends on what high school the student attends. College admittance boards know the reputation of various high schools, especially those in their area. When I was a member of college admission boards, the committee knew some private high schools overinflated grades, and some public schools passed students who could barely read or write. We also knew which schools had diplomas that were not worth the paper they were printed on and which schools helped students pass standardized tests. I had students in my college classes who had difficulty reading at the fifth-grade level. This is why standardized tests were so important because they assisted the selection committee in grade validation.

There has been a great deal of discussion on the use of standardized tests. Still, the ACT/SAT verifies and calibrates grand point averages (GPAs) and identifies a potential student's weak academic areas. Can a student have a 3.5 GPA and bomb the ACT? Yes, it is possible, and some students have test anxiety. Still, it is unlikely that a student with a GPA above 3.5 from a school with a reputation for rigorous academic standards will score below 18 on the ACT. When this happens, we suspect the high school over-inflates the grades or the students have another issue, possibly a medical diagnosis or a learning disorder. Usually, a student will take the ACT more than once, and scores rise with each attempt, but if the score remains the same and the student has a high GPA, boards suspect it is a case of grade inflation or the high school has low academic standards. I have also seen academic institutions that do not use grades but instead give group projects. While this approach can develop team building, it can also hide an ill-equipped student who isn't doing their share of the academic work. Therefore, it's important to understand how and where the grades originate.

Many colleges will accept students with a low ACT/SAT score or optional ACT/SATs, but remember, colleges are there to make money, so just because they accept the student does not mean the student will graduate. The university pays tuition whether the student passes or fails a class. I recommend looking for schools with high graduation and retention rates because if both are low at a four-year university, this may not be an institution of higher learning that focuses on student success. I felt it was a disservice to both the parents and the student to accept a student with an ACT below 16. In my experience, I have yet to see a student with an aggregate score of 16 or below graduate from a four-year college without attending community college first. The exception is the student attending Community College before transferring to a four-year university. A Community

College, which usually has open enrollment, can assist the students in developing the academic and study skills they may not have acquired in high school. It's essential to note retention rates at community colleges may appear low, but the community college may have a high transfer rate to four-year institutions.

Is it the end of the world if a student can't score high enough to get into the college of their choice? No, because poor standardized test takers may be able to take advantage of "Super Scoring," which allows students to capitalize on areas of the exam where they are strong and use those scores to raise their overall ACT/SAT score.

CHAPTER 3

SUPER SCORING ON THE ACT/SAT

Not all universities allow "super scoring' on standardized tests, but some do. Super scoring enables the university to consider the student's score on a given section during the entire testing period of the standardized test. This allows the student to focus on the composite score instead of each section simultaneously. This process allows a student to retake the ACT/SAT numerous times, and the highest score from a given category will count in that category even if the student scores lower on subsequent exams. Example: If the student scored a 21 in the Math area the first time they took the ACT but an 18 in Math the second time but scored a 21 in English the first time and a 17 the second time, the college will accept the higher scores in the categories from previous or later attempts. This process allows the student to focus on one area each time they take the ACT/SAT; however, since the ACT is not free, there is a cost every time the student takes the exam. There is also a minimum waiting period between exams. However, this method may allow a student who is excellent in Math but poor in English to raise each score individually while taking the test numerous times over a longer period. The university website or college admission page should annotate if they accept Super Scoring. If you are still unsure, ask the admittance counselor.

The COVID-19 pandemic made colleges reevaluate the standardized testing system, and as a result, some colleges do not require the ACT/SAT, or it may be optional. A student can also take a practice SAT/ACT without reporting the scores to a university. I recommend taking these tests in middle school, and many schools provide practice exams at little to no cost. However, if students do well, they can leverage this score to gain pre-admittance to some universities. Some colleges have summer programs for students who scored well on the pre-SAT because they want to cultivate a relationship with a potential future student. My daughter took a college class at her future college while still a high school student at an "Early College Program." Research summer programs for high school and middle school students.

Suppose none of these methods assist the student in obtaining admission to a four-year university. In that case, there is still open enrollment at most Community Colleges and Historically Black Colleges and Universities (HBCUs). Community Colleges are the best value for all college students and their families. I recommend students consider attending at least one year at a Community College in their area. Historically Black Colleges and Universities also provide many opportunities for all students because they have traditional four-year degree programs and may have scholarships available for non-minority students.

CHAPTER 4

THE MIRACLE OF COMMUNITY COLLEGES

An excellent way to level the playing field for students who may need more skills to succeed in more rigorous university programs is the miracle of Community Colleges. Community Colleges allow students to improve their higher education academic skills at a lower cost than most four-year institutions, and they provide an excellent alternative for students to complete their core classes (English, History, etc.) without spending money for courses that have nothing to do with a student's major field of study at expensive universities. Most universities require all students complete a core curriculum. This requirement is usually 30 semester hours and encompasses English, Literature, Algebra, History, Social Science (Psychology and Sociology), and Core Sciences like Biology or Chemistry. While these are useful courses, taking them constitutes almost 30 hours of courses most students take in high school. Some classes may even use the same books as the high school class. These core classes can let students explore various fields of study before they select a major, but if a student is focused on what they want to do and study, these classes can be costly time-consuming, distraction. Also, in my experience, some departments make these courses much more complicated than needed, or they have graduate teaching assistants with little to no teaching experience. I would avoid a class taught by a graduate assistant or review the professor's history on "ratemyprofessor.com" to ensure the course is not more difficult than needed because failing or a poor grade in a core class can devastate a GPA.

Community colleges offer core requirements like English, History, Algebra, Literature, Biology, etc. The student can complete required courses at a third of the cost of major universities. These colleges also allow less academically mature students to develop the necessary study and test-taking skills to complete a Bachelor's Degree. However, once again, the student must ensure the credits transfer from the Community College to the four-year institution. Before enrolling in a community college, ensure the credits from those courses will transfer to the four-year university by contacting the registrar. Most universities compare the course description, syllabus, and credit hours when considering whether the classes and credits will transfer. The closer the course description is to the other university's description of the same class, the more likely the credits will transfer. However, some programs require you to take specific courses or a number of credit hours at the degree-granting four-year university. These requirements should be listed on the university website, but if you have a question, contact the registrar's office for clarification and get a written response. Remember, course and major requirements change, and colleges may have personnel turnover in key positions. Ensure you have everything in writing from the registrar if you have questions or check with the Dean of Academic Affairs.

The registrar is the expert on credit hour transfers.I would not contact the college advisor because they do not have the authority on what transfers, nor can they grant credit or make substitutions for courses. Even a professor in a given area is not an expert in transfer credits. As stated earlier, people frequently change positions in academia, and if one registrar states the college will accept the credits from the community college and a new registrar and their office does not accept the transfer credits, you will have an audit trail. You can raise the issue with the Dean of Students or Provost, so ensure you have it in writing, which includes an email. Do not be afraid to raise or take these issues to a higher authority. If you don't ask, the answer is always no. A college would prefer you take another class or retake a similar class because it generates tuition.

Another common practice from four-year universities is to accept credits but not GPAs from other institutions or community colleges. If the student has a 3.5 GPA and sixty credit hours, which usually constitute an Associate's Degree, the four-year university may accept the credit hours but not the GPA. This can be a blessing and a grade point saver when taking a challenging class. A grade of "D" is a passing grade and will provide the credits unless the college specifically states a specific grade must be obtained for transfer credit. Also, ensure the four-year college will accept classes with a grade below a "C." I know some four-year universities will not accept any English or Literature grade below a "B" from a community college, which means the student does not get the credit hours for the class and will need to repeat the course. If a course is part of the major, like Calculus for engineering, the four-year college may not accept anything below a "C." Verify before you take the class.

CHAPTER 5

OPEN ENROLLMENT COLLEGES AND TRANSFER STUDENTS

A s stated earlier, not all high schools are the same, and not all universities are created equally. Just because everyone can get into college does not mean everyone should attend college. However, if you want to attend college, there is always a university willing to take you and your money. Some universities have waived college entrance exams like the ACT/SAT, while other universities will admit students with ACT scores below 18, which is considered an acceptable but low ACT score. Average ACT scores fluctuate, but most public schools hover around twenty-one, while average private schools may average closer to twenty-five. Since not all high school grades are equal, the standardized tests provide a baseline for academic measurement, and a minimum composite score of 18 on the ACT or 1200 on the SAT will gain admission to most average state universities. Some universities and colleges do not require standardized tests and minimum high school GPAs for admittance; those universities are usually called "**open enrollment**" universities. This does not mean the college is not academically rigorous or has lower standards; it just means they have different enrollment requirements to be accepted as a student. A student could also be accepted on a probationary status during their first semester. Usually, the student must take a "College Success" course that includes the basics of study skills, writing, and math. It may also include life skills like balancing courses and social activities and may include additional access to resources on campus like tutors and mentors to facilitate academic success.

Open enrollment institutions are an excellent starting point if you want to attend another university but do not meet the minimum requirements. For most major universities, once you have 30 credit hours on the semester systems and a 2.5 GPA, you can transfer to the college of your choice. However, the 30 hours usually must include one English, History, Social Science, and Math course.

As a transfer student, you are in a completely different category than a high school graduate trying to gain admittance to a four-year college. If you live away from home and are no longer dependent on your parents' income, you are also in a different category for financial aid. In most circumstances, you would become eligible for financial aid if your income is below the poverty level. Many students would be eligible for Pell Grants or other financial aid because they would be under the poverty threshold for financial eligibility.

One loophole in receiving financial aid is emancipating your student before applying to college. This may be an option if your family income is too high to qualify for financial aid, but paying for a student to attend college would present a financial burden. This legal and financial matter could influence your taxes, medical coverage, and other issues, so it is advisable to consult a lawyer and certified public accountant before implementing this option. If the student is still living at home with their parents and the parents are providing over 50% of their support, they would be considered dependents for tax reasons, but if the parents do not need to take the standard tax dependent deduction, let the student live on their own for six months, don't declare them on your taxes. They will most likely qualify for financial aid if their income is below the poverty threshold. Once again, consult with an attorney and accountant, but this has been a successful tactic to help students pay for college.

Another excellent resource to pay for college is the military. I am a military veteran and used the Army to pay for two master's degrees and my doctorate. While this option may not appeal to everyone, there are some loopholes or ways to manipulate the system to pay for college but not serve in the military.

CHAPTER 6

MILITARY ACADEMIES AND RESERVE OFFICER TRAINING SCHOOL (ROTC)

All services (Army, Navy, Air Force, Coast Guard, and Merchant Marines) have service academies. The Space Force usually attends the Air Force Academy. Acceptance to these academies is competitive and requires a six-year obligation to stay in the service. However, most people do not know students have **no obligation** to serve in the military until they begin their junior year of college. *This means the first two years of college are on Uncle Sam.* At the end of the sophomore year, a student can transfer to another college debt-free without obligation to join the military. The same applies to the Reserve Officer Training Program (ROTC) for the different military services. The services do not advertise this fact, but until the student is a contracted cadet beginning their junior year, they have no obligation to serve in the military.

Depending on the university, it may or may not have a ROTC program for each service. Smaller colleges may have satellite ROTC programs operating outside a more prominent university. Southern Union Community College in Alabama falls under Auburn University's ROTC program; Capital University falls under Ohio State University, so students may have to drill or take other classes at the more prominent university while attending smaller institutions. This is an excellent way to select the military service of your choice and still attend the university of choice. Most of these programs are within close proximity to the smaller colleges. Like the service academies, students are not obligated to join the military until they contract with ROTC in their junior year. The services also don't advertise that students can take a ROTC class in their freshmen and sophomore years. These classes are usually easy A's and teach basic leadership skills. Some universities do not accept the credit hours from ROTC and treat them as electives. Instructors are usually active duty military or government contractors and may not have teaching credentials or doctoral degrees, which could also influence the accreditation of the programs at the university.

Each university is different, and some universities require ROTC faculty to possess advanced degrees, so do your homework before enrolling in an ROTC class. If your major requires 120 hours for graduation, the ROTC classes may add another twenty hours to your degree program, and adding these courses could add another semester to college. If you have an ROTC scholarship or are a contracted cadet, which means you are obligated to serve in the military, the ROTC scholarships will cover books and tuition. Some universities even provide free room and board for ROTC scholarship students. Students also get a monthly stipend, which varies by service but averages $450 monthly and is increased yearly. ROTC also offers specific scholarships for nursing students and other specialty degrees.

There are different types of ROTC scholarships. Some are national, and others are university-based. Each service's website will detail these types of scholarships. In national scholarships, a student is awarded a scholarship through the service and can attend any university of their choice if they are accepted and if it has an ROTC program. The university may also award scholarships in conjunction with an ROTC scholarship, like free room and board.

Each university and service has a set number of scholarships, so if you are interested in an ROTC scholarship, the student should apply at the beginning of their high school senior year, but I recommend contacting the ROTC offices at the college the student wants to attend during the junior year of high school. Each college also has four, three, and two-year scholarships, so if students don't receive one in their freshmen or sophomore year, they could still receive one for their junior and senior years. Many scholarships also pay for room and board, but it varies by university.

When the competition was tough, four-year ROTC scholarships were difficult to obtain, but since the military began having difficulty recruiting, the process of gaining a scholarship became much easier, especially for larger services like the Army and Navy. Students who do well in freshmen year ROTC classes but are not on scholarship are often recruited by the services to accept a ROTC scholarship. However, there is no obligation to serve in the military until a student begins their junior year as a contracted cadet. Another little-known service is the Uniformed Public Health Service (UPHS), which wears uniforms similar to the Navy and recruits health professionals but is not part of the Department of Defense. Another service similar to the military is the National Oceanic and Atmospheric Administration (NOAA), which recruits pilots and other professionals for research and scientific exploration of the oceans. The UPHS and NOAA provide an opportunity to serve the public without the dangers of being in the military. The UPHS also recruits for its medical school, which is another option for students seeking a career in medicine.

TRUE STORY: When I was working in Army ROTC recruiting, our ROTC department of the college awarded a four-year nursing scholarship to a freshman student working to obtain her Bachelor of Science in Nursing. The Army ROTC scholarship paid for everything, including her stethoscope, lab equipment, tuition, books, room and board, and a generous monthly stipend. At the end of her four years and after she passed her nursing exam (which the Army funded), she was commissioned a 2nd Lieutenant in the Army. The same week, she suddenly developed a medical condition, sleepwalking. Since soldiers are not deployable if they sleepwalk, she was given a medical discharge. If a service member has a medical discharge, they are not responsible for paying back the ROTC scholarships unless fraud or a concealed medical condition is found. She passed her medical exam before being commissioned, so it would have been difficult to prove she had a preexisting condition. She did not have to pay back any scholarship money, had all four years of college paid for, and graduated debt-free and she secured a position at one of the local hospitals. She found the loophole and had no intention of serving in the Army. The primary military (PMS) instructor was furious, but I congratulated her and said, "Nicely played." She never admitted to playing the system, but considering she developed her medical condition immediately after graduation, one can assume she had done her research. If the Army does not like the results, the service should close the loopholes.

Another loophole is gaining "veteran status" to receive Pell Grants and other veteran benefits. The obvious way is to enlist in the military and serve your initial term of enlistment, which ranges from four to six years. Yet, if a person enlists in the military and, while at basic training, gets hurt or has some other medical condition that leads to an honorable discharge, which is the characterization of a medical discharge, they will receive veterans benefits once discharged. There is one caveat to this: the service member must have over 180 days of service. If they have under 180 days, they can receive an Initial Entry Discharge (IED), basically like saying they were never in the military. An IED discharge is neither honorable nor dishonorable; it is uncharacterized but does not grant veteran benefits. Therefore, if a student joins the military and is hurt after 180 days of service and develops a medical condition like a chronic knee or back problem due to physical activity or some other military training-related physical issue that caused a medical problem, they will be discharged. If the condition renders the student non-deployable or precludes military duties, like exercise-induced asthma, they may receive a medical discharge and other compensation. Concealing a known medical condition is illegal and could lead to a dishonorable discharge. Obviously, this will require some medical documentation, but like the ROTC nursing student, some things are more difficult to diagnose or prove.

I have known service members to receive medical discharges for flat feet, shin splints, or broken arms. Some who received medical discharges currently receive Veterans Administration (VA) disability pay and veteran benefits like free college tuition and guaranteed home loans. I also know veterans who receive VA disability pay for having a hysterectomy or gall bladder removed because the loss of an organ usually receives 30-50% VA disability, which currently equates to $1,000.00 a month tax-free for the rest of their lives. The rate changes each year based on inflation and the federal budget. The system is flawed, but it is the system. If you have veteran status, you will likely receive some college financial benefits, including the G.I. Bill, which pays for tuition and living expenses. If the student is the child of 100% disabled veterans, there are additional benefits like Chapter 35, which provides a monthly stipend to the student while they are enrolled in college. These benefits change, so it's advisable to research the VA website for specifics about each benefit available to veterans' dependents.

A dependent child does not have to live with the service member to obtain dependent benefits. Do not confuse dependent veteran benefits with veteran benefits. A dependent is the child or spouse of a veteran. A veteran is someone who served in the military and usually has an honorable discharge.

If you are eighteen years old, living with your parents, and have veteran status, the FASFA system treats you as an emancipated adult, and you do not have to declare your parent's income in FASFA. However, you must include your tax statements, so ensure you file your taxes yearly, regardless of income. FASFA does a cross-check in their system with income tax records. The income tax filings are used to verify income for both the student and the parents to determine the level of financial aid.

The military can provide an excellent opportunity for those who wish to serve, and it will pay and provide an outstanding education, but it's not for everyone. Also, not everyone qualifies to serve in the military. Each service has slightly different admission standards, but height/weight requirements and the ability to obtain a security clearance are prerequisites for all services. In addition, physical fitness standards, and aptitude requirements are also dependent on the service. Currently, less than 25% of the population of the United States meets the minimum standards to join the military. As recruiting becomes more difficult, these standards may change, and a military recruiter or the ROTC department at the college can assist with the process of joining the military. The student should weigh their options before joining the military, but the services provide unique opportunities to fund college and an exciting career.

CHAPTER 7

SAVE MONEY WITH COLLEGE LEVEL EXAMINATIONS (CLEP) AND ADVANCE PLACEMENT EXAMS

Another way to save tuition money is by enrolling in Advance Placement (AP) high school courses or taking College Level Examination Programs (CLEP) exams. CLEP tests are a credit-by-examination program that measures a student's comprehension of introductory college-level material. The approved list of approved CLEP exams is available on most college websites, but some colleges, like Auburn University, do not accept CLEP exams. CLEP exams are free to military members but cost, on average, $150.00. This is still significantly less expensive than paying for a three or four-credit class. History, English, and Psychology are popular CLEP exams and, according to feedback on the CLEP websites, are easier to pass than Algebra, Calculus, or Physics CLEP exams. Are CLEP exams easy to pass? The answer is it depends on the student.

Most colleges require placement exams for Math and English unless the student scores high enough on the ACT/SAT. If a student does not want to take an introductory Math prep course, which may not award credit, I recommend studying for a CLEP exam or taking AP Algebra in high school.

Online study guides are available for all CLEP exams, and exams must be taken at a proctored test center. A student can retake a CLEP exam until it is passed, but most retests require 90 days between each attempt. Advance Placement (AP) exams are similar and are conducted after a student takes an AP course in high school. AP Exams are standardized exams designed to measure how well a student mastered the content and skills of a specific AP course. Most AP courses have an end-of-year exam, which also comes with a cost, but a few courses have different assessments. Art and Design courses may allow students to submit a portfolio for scoring. I knew a student who CLEPed their entire freshmen and sophomore year and most of their core requirements. He then transferred to a state college with 62 credit hours and cut the cost of a college degree in half. This may not be the norm, but it is attainable, and students can take CLEP exams while still in high school. Attempting the CLEP exams after taking a similar high school course may make the content easier to recall. Base Education Centers will usually administer the CLEP exams for military members and their dependents.

Before taking a CLEP exam, please verify with the university registrar's office that they will take the exam results for a given course and add the credit hours to the student's transcripts. CLEP exams do not come with a grade, just a pass or fail, and provide the student with the credit hours associated with the course. Some majors may not allow students to use CLEP exams for credit, so ensure the student verifies that the exam is accepted. AP course credit is usually accepted by most colleges depending on the minimum score requirements for the subject.

CHAPTER 8

USE CORE REQUIREMENTS AND DUAL ENROLLMENT TO GRADUATE EARLY

I mentioned "Core Requirements" earlier, but all potential college students must understand the core requirements and the required classes to meet the standard. Each four-year university should list what classes constitute these requirements. Usually, this includes 6 hours of a History in sequence, ex. Western History I and Western History II and one Literature or 6 hours of Literature in sequence and one History. If you're better at history, I recommend taking two history classes and one literature class or vice versa. Core requirements include 4 hours of science, like Biology or Chemistry, but they may also offer Biology for non-majors, Astronomy, or Geology. A social science degree like Psychology, Sociology, or Anthropology is also required, as well as a Fine Arts course like Music or Art Appreciation. Some universities may offer Architecture Appreciation as a choice, and my university offered a course called History of Films, where we watched classic movies that counted for

Fine Art credit. It was actually very informative and fun. Math requirements like Algebra or Pre-Calculus are also required, and some universities offer a course called Finite Math, which is well suited for mathematically challenged students. However, depending on the major, a student may still be required to take another math course like Statistics.

The best advice is to study what constitutes the Core Requirements at your university and make choices based on your interests. If you are worried it could adversely impact your GPA, take the courses best suited for academic success. As stated earlier, most core requirements are basically a repeat of classes taken in high school and sometimes may be the same class. Core requirements usually consist of between 30-60 credit hours, and now, some colleges require Women's Studies or a diversity course. In my opinion, it would be more beneficial to require finance and economics courses and a "How to Fill Out a Job Application" course. A lesson on US government, Economics, and Constitutional Law might also be helpful, but every university is different, so do your research on required courses.

Instead of spending money on these courses at the university, which could be a very expensive review of high school classes, take the core requirements during high school at a Community College or through CLEP tests or **dual enrollment.** If the high school offers "dual enrollment," this allows high school juniors and seniors to take classes at a local college for both high school and college credit, for a discounted fee. If done correctly, a student can graduate from high school with an Associate's Degree from a local community college, which saves two years of tuition and allows the student to focus on their primary degree requirements. If your high school does not have a dual enrollment program, ask if they could begin one. Usually, the local college will accept reduced tuition to fill classes.

CHAPTER 9

UNIVERSITY ADVISORS

Many people in university advising positions are not experts in the particular area where they advise. Most of the advisors at large universities are recent college graduates looking for a "starter job," and advising is an open university position they could use to move on to something else. Advisors may be graduate students augmenting their income or as part of a scholarship, and some advisors do not have degrees or work in the field where they are acting as advisors.

The university where I worked used the administrative staff as advisors, and none of the advisors had degrees in the area. This does not mean they don't know the degree requirements; most of them use a spreadsheet and course handbook to complete the degree requirements, which most of the time will suffice. However, courses change, handbooks are updated, and students need to be aware of the changing environment.

True Story: *The advisor for my daughter for the Communicative Disorders program was not a Communicative*

Disorders major and never applied to a graduate Speech Pathology Program. She provided bad guidance on a course that did not count toward graduation requirements, resulting in an additional class and increased cost before graduation. The advisor was also unaware of the observation hours required to be competitive for graduate school. As a result, she had to shadow a Speech Language Pathologist over the summer to meet the required observation hours.

This is a typical story if you speak with students and parents. Suppose the advisor for pre-med students isn't a medical doctor or other professional working in the field. In that case, I recommend that the student find someone at the university who practices in the field and ask them for additional advice on course selection. Some professors are former practitioners in the area where they teach, so find a professor who has worked in the field where the student is studying and seek his/her advice. Also, remember the standards and degree requirements change. For example, during the COVID-19 pandemic, the GRE was suspended for some graduate programs. The LSAT is no longer required for some law schools, and the recent implementation of diversity, inclusion, and equity into academia continues to change the standards, requirements, and graduation criteria. It is in your best interest to keep up with the changes, and this book will outline the "truth at the time," so do your research and ensure you know the specifics of your college and program of study.

CHAPTER 10

GRADUATING IN FOUR YEARS

The new norm is for college students to graduate in five years. To graduate from most programs, which require 120 credit hours, students will have to average 15 hours a semester. A course load of 12 hours is required to be considered a full-time student and receive most benefits associated with full-time enrollment, like grants, student loans, and some veterans benefits. In the summer, the requirement is different. Usually, only seven hours are required in the summer to be considered a full-time student. In addition, it is common for a student to drop a class if they are failing or get closed out of a required class during registration. These factors result in many students taking less than twelve hours a semester. Some universities offer a flat rate per semester, including 12-18 credits. Depending on the student's GPA, they may require advisor or faculty approval to take over fifteen hours. My undergraduate college offered this option, so I always took at least fifteen hours because I wanted to get the most out of college for the money. I would have graduated early, but I changed my major and needed the entire four years to meet the requirements of my new major. Instead of overloading a student with too many credits, another way to ensure a student can graduate in four years is to take classes in the summer.

Summer Enrollment

Not all courses are offered during the summer term, and summer classes are usually eight weeks in length instead of the usual fourteen—to sixteen-week semester. The material presented in eight weeks may be the same as during the longer semesters, so students should be prepared to work quickly and diligently over the summer. However, a student may also find less material presented in a summer class.

As stated previously, being considered a full-time student in the summer usually requires only six to eight credit hours. This can be important when calculating Student Aid or other benefits. Regardless, if your student wants to graduate in four years, the best course of action is to consider completing one or two semesters over the summer. As explained in the next section, the courses can also be taken at another college, like a Community College.

Transient Student Status

It is typical for freshmen, sophomore, and even junior-status students to get closed out of popular or high-demand classes, depending on the major. This may result in the student being unable to complete a prerequisite course. They need to register for another class. In addition, this class may only be offered once a year in a particular semester. Therefore, the student would have to wait another year to enroll in the course. An example would be Principles of Accounting I, which would be needed for Principles of Accounting II, or

Pre-Calculus, which would be required for Calculus. This could prevent graduation within four years. An excellent way to stay on track to graduate in four years is to attend another college as a transient student.

As a transient student, you are still enrolled at your primary college but taking classes at another university. This is also helpful if a class is known to have a difficult instructor and another university offers an alternative instructor. The tuition is paid to the other university where the class is taken, but the credits and sometimes the grade will also transfer. However, not all universities take transient credits, and their registrar's homepage should have a link to the transient form, which will verify whether the class at the other university will transfer toward the degree at the primary university. Also, most colleges require at least forty-five to sixty credits to be taken at the primary university to receive a diploma from that university. Each college is different, so verify before registering as a transient student at another university.

Another advantage of "transient student status" is that scholarships, veteran benefits, and other amenities associated with the parent college remain in effect. Suppose a student transfers between different colleges and their four-year college each semester. In that case, they may have to reapply for admittance, which creates a new set of problems each semester when grants and scholarships must also be transferred. A "transient" form prevents this confusion and allows students to take classes at other universities while remaining at their parent university. However, ensure the degree program accepts all the credits from other institutions. In addition, some degrees have a maximum number of transferred credits allowed, so once again, check with the registrar and the university website, which will have a link to a transient form.

Night Classes

Sometimes, students cannot fit a class into their schedule during the "normal" academic day. Most colleges offer courses after 5 pm and since these classes may cater to non-traditional or working students, they are sometimes less academically rigorous then day classes. Professors recognize that some students take night classes because they have full-time jobs or maybe take care of family members while attending college part-time or full-time to complete a degree or get additional training for a promotion or a career change. Taking classes with more "mature" or working students can provide an excellent example for teenage college students. Non-traditional students usually pay for the classes themselves or are reimbursed by work to take courses, unlike some college students, who may not have a vested financial interest because they are not paying the tuition or trying to get a promotion.

It was beneficial to team a younger traditional day student with a non-traditional night student in group projects because the non-traditional student brings experience and maturity to the class. In contrast, the teenage student may have better study and computer skills. Non-traditional students may also have better time management skills since they juggle work, family, and college. Night classes also provide a convenience for students working and supplementing their income to pay for college, room and board, or other college expenses.

CHAPTER 11

ON-CAMPUS HOUSING VS OFF-CAMPUS HOUSING

Although it may seem illogical, on-campus housing, on average, is more expensive than living off-campus. Students are housed on university property and pay mandatory meal plans so students eat at university dining facilities. They may also pay costly parking fees to park on campus near their dorms. Most college websites will summarize the cost of living on and off campus. It can be a cost versus convenience comparison. On-campus housing may offer the convenience of walking to class, proximity to dining facilities, and access to on-campus resources like libraries, study groups, and extra-curricular activities. However, if cost is not a consideration, I recommend that students live on campus during their freshmen year because they can better appreciate the college experience and build social relationships. Most on-campus housing requires a student to live with roommates unless they want a private room at an additional cost. Sharing a room with a stranger, learning how to manage their time and classes, and living on their own for the first time can be challenging, but it is also a chance to mature. Some students have never lived away from home, and there is an extra level of security and supervision in on-campus housing. How many parents followed the school bus or sat in the parking lot when their children entered kindergarten? We can't do this to college-aged children, but knowing they are in a secure building, staffed with security, can alleviate some parental angst.

Most dorms have resident assistants (RA) who are upperclassmen and live in the dorms with the students and are there to enforce curfews and other campus rules. They also can monitor students who may have difficulty adjusting to college life and academics and provide resources for students who need help in these areas. I recommend touring the on-campus housing options because they are not all equal. When I was in college, campus housing was a tiny room with two twin beds and a built-in desk, chair, and small closet. My roommate and I were very creative on how to make additional space, and the bed was built into the wall so it couldn't be raised for extra space or as drawers under the bed. Depending on the university, the dorms are nicer than my first apartment. In addition, some universities have "Honor's College Housing," and if the student qualifies for this housing, they are usually much nicer than the regular dorms. I also recommend that freshman students live with another freshman. Misery loves company, but it's an integral part of the socialization process. College can be stressful, and it's better to have another person to share experiences, good and bad, and provide support when the student is away from family and friends.

Tour the dorms in person. The older the dorm, the more likely it will lack modern conveniences and have larger spaces. Older buildings and facilities can present challenges like one or two elevators, limited bathrooms, and less than optimal HVAC systems. Expect your student to get ill in the first semester of college because of the proximity to living with other students. Most new college students need to be more adept at keeping their dorm rooms clean, eating a balanced meal, and getting enough sleep. Janitorial services are outsourced, but they do not clean the students' rooms and usually do not clean common areas daily. If the university offers a laundry service, I recommend signing up for it during the first semester of college. While it may seem expensive, it's cheaper than replacing stolen or damaged clothing from inadequate community washers and dryers. In addition, laundry will not be a priority for new freshmen as they try to balance classes, parties, and living independently.

Off-campus housing can provide opportunities for students to learn life skills like paying rent and utilities, cleaning their rooms and common areas, and commuting to class. On average, off-campus housing is less expensive, and students usually have more choices, like condos, homes, apartments, and even subletting from another renter. Off-campus housing can be furnished, unfurnished, or a combination of both. However, renters should be aware that most off-campus housing requires students to sign a lease for the entire academic year, including part of the summer. Large real estate corporations may own multiple properties, making it difficult, if not impossible, for a renter to break a lease even if the leasing agency does not fulfill its duties. They may also charge above average amounts for utilities, furniture rental, and other incidentals like trash pick-up and internet. If a student lives off-campus, do your research before signing a lease. Just like the dorms, personally visit and ask to see an apartment or condo in the facility. Ask questions about how to remove a less-than-desirable roommate who would be responsible for the rent and the criteria and consequences for breaking a lease. I have seen leasing companies fail to fix broken plumbing or provide amenities like study rooms and a gym but continue to charge the students full rent. Also, most companies do not rent by the condo or apartment but by the room. If the rent is $1000 monthly for a two-bedroom apartment, that may not mean each student pays $500, but each student pays $1000. Clarify the costs before signing any lease and look for hidden expenses like mandatory rental insurance purchased through the apartment complex, internet, cable, and minimum costs for water and electricity.

Parking can also be an issue when living on and off campus, so explore the costs of a parking pass and the proximity to your classes. Some campuses offer less expensive parking passes to military, veterans, and dependents of veterans. The university VA office can outline the benefits for eligible students. They may also offer discounted books, tutoring, or other benefits regardless of on or off-campus status.

Sororities and Fraternities

I was in a sorority, and they also provided an excellent alternative to housing. Some universities have fraternity and sorority houses where members of the organization can reside. Usually, this is open to members after their freshmen year. Many of these organizations have beautiful mansions with gorgeous architecture and furnishings and private chefs with kitchens that provide three meals daily, which could be much less expensive and more nutritious than on-campus meal plans. However, the cost associated with joining a fraternity or sorority may offset any savings from living in the houses.

Not all sorority and fraternity houses are equal. Some houses are located on-campus and considered college property, so there may be additional restrictions to living there. Some houses are off campus and may need to be in a better state of repair. Also, some organizations have strict rules about alcohol consumption and grades. If a member violates a policy, they can be separated from the organization and immediately evicted from the house. There are no refunds if a member is kicked out of the organization. If members don't pay their dues on time, they can be evicted from the house. Also, sororities and fraternities may have to "fill" their house to pay the bills and mortgage, so they can require members to live in the house if not enough members volunteer. From personal experience, this is much more expensive than living anywhere else on or off campus. However, it does provide a level of security, convenience to campus, and usually decent food.

My university had sections of the dorm for sorority members. If you belonged to the sorority, you could live in that dorm, which had a nice Chapter Room and common area for studying. Back in the 1980s, it was primarily used for parties. It was just like a regular dorm, but only members of the sorority lived there, and we followed additional rules associated with our sorority. Each university is different, so research the organization's requirements.

True Story: *The large university in Alabama has a myriad of off-campus housing owned by a corporation from Colorado.*

A roommate's boyfriend committed suicide in the apartment, and the other roommate was forced to live there until the apartment rented out the empty room. The same complex charged $50 a month for used rental furniture. The parents of the young man who killed himself had to clean the room, and the corporation kept the girlfriend's security deposit when she moved out and left school. This same apartment complex closed all common areas, which included the gym, study rooms, complimentary coffee bar, security, and suspended trash pick-up and maintenance. More than one apartment had plumbing problems. Someone was assaulted on the grounds because they failed to provide security, as promised in the lease. When a couple of students notified the apartment complex they were moving out, the apartment complex took the students to court for breaking the lease. One of the student's relatives was a lawyer who represented the student in court. The student was able to prove the apartment complex broke the lease agreement first and won the case, but it would have been more expensive if the student had to pay a lawyer. The apartment complex assumed the renter would not take this route because it would cost more than paying the outstanding rent, and they would win a summary judgment against the student, who most likely cannot afford to hire a lawyer or would not be present for their court date. This was not the case; the student documented the safety and maintenance problems. The case was dismissed because the apartment complex did not present any evidence on their behalf. Read the lease carefully and know your rights if the rental agency or owner does not provide what is promised in the lease.

Despite potential problems with landlords, living off-campus is still less expensive if the housing is close to campus. Meals account for a large portion of the expenses of on-campus housing, and since the dorms rarely have kitchens for safety reasons, they prohibit students from cooking in their rooms. Off-campus housing can allow students to save money by cooking their meals. Also, if they live off campus, they can usually obtain a commuter parking permit, which tends to be much less expensive than the parking passes for students who live on campus.

Regardless of where the student lives, I recommend obtaining renter's insurance, as many on- and off-campus residences require renter's insurance. In addition, although most off-campus housing has locks on the individual bedroom doors, invest in a wall safe where students can lock up their valuables. Alarm systems and cameras, like "Ring," can also provide additional security. Also, ensure the parking lot has adequate lighting and security. Most crime in off-campus housing is related to vehicle break-ins and theft of contents left in vehicles. Thieves know students have computers, iPads, and cell phones, easily pawned items. Criminals also know students sometimes live out of their cars and may not want to carry everything to class. Do not make your vehicle an easy target, and do not leave valuables visible in your car or apartment.

CHAPTER 12

IN-STATE TUITION VS OUT-OF-STATE TUITION

Most public universities offer in-state tuition to students who live in the same state as the institution. On average, tuition to a state college is 2 to 3 times less expensive for a resident. To prove in-state residency, colleges require parents and students to provide various forms of proof, which may include tax records, W-2s, rental agreements, property taxes, voter registration, driver's license, vehicle plates, and utility bills from the past two years. If your college of choice is out-of-state, research the time limit to become an in-state resident and whether it may be advantageous to transfer to the college after meeting the instate requirements. Each institution is different, so research the requirements before applying for in-state tuition. There may also be some exceptions for military students, their families, and spouses, or international students.

If you are attending a state college and are not a state resident, expect to pay much higher tuition, but it can also increase your chances of acceptance since state colleges can charge higher tuition rates for out-of-state students. Therefore, paying more money could increase your chances of attending a college of your choice if it is in another state. Most out-of-state students need to realize they can apply for in-state tuition once they have lived there for two years, so if you attend an out-of-state college at the end of your sophomore year, you may qualify for in-state tuition. Check the residency requirements and work toward obtaining those documents to lower the cost of tuition.

Although most accept federal and state funds, private universities usually have a set tuition price regardless of in or out-of-state residency. Many private universities offer generous scholarship opportunities, which could make them less expensive than larger public colleges, so do your research and cost analysis. I attended a private liberal arts school in Ohio because it was much cheaper than the state universities due to the number of grants, work-study programs, and scholarships. Obtaining a scholarship from a smaller private school with fewer students may also be less competitive than a large university. A decision matrix can be an excellent tool to compare costs at public, private, in-state, and out-of-state universities, and the various criteria at the top of the matrix can be changed based on each student.

	Tuition Costs	Books Costs	Room and Board Costs	(Scholarships)	(Student Aid/Work Study)
In state Public University					
Out of State Public University					
In state Private University					
Out of state Private University					
Total Costs:					

Cost should not be the only consideration when attending a university. Finding a viable, well-paying job in their area of study is usually the goal of most college graduates. Most universities offer resume writing, internships, and job placement services. Students should visit these areas and look at the hiring rates for recent graduates in the same major they will study. Universities track these statistics, and if the average graduate from the university is 98% likely to be employed above median pay for that profession within three months after graduation, the college may be an excellent choice.

Employers and graduate schools know the colleges that produce a quality product, and students are the product. Attend a college that produces a quality graduate because after four years, or more, in college and a cost of close to

$100,000, the student should be able to find a job. Although the field of study plays a significant role in the hiring process, the goal of graduation is to get a job or be accepted to graduate school.

If the student must attend graduate school to complete their career goals, acceptance rates to graduate school for the program is an important consideration. Also, some colleges don't offer all programs. If the university you want to attend doesn't offer an architecture program, it's a bad idea to attend that university if you want to be an architect. While some professional degrees like law and dentistry may accept various undergraduate programs, most master's programs require mandatory undergraduate courses, so ensure the undergraduate school offers those courses. If you don't like your field of study after the first semester or year, you can still change your major, but it may increase cost due to additional semesters to graduate.

CHAPTER 13

CHANGING YOUR MAJOR (DON'T DO IT... AFTER YOUR SOPHOMORE YEAR)

It is unlikely that recent high school graduates will know precisely what they want to study when they attend college. I am still struggling with this decision, which is probably why my undergraduate degree, master's degree, and doctorate are all in different disciplines. Suppose a student is positive and wants to become a doctor. In that case, most universities have a pre-med academic track, and they would register for Biology (for majors), Chemistry, Calculus, and take a Psychology course to satisfy the social science requirement. After taking Psychology, the student may decide to major in Psychology and become a Social Worker. If this decision is reached during the first semester, the student is still on the path to graduate in four years. However, if in the middle of the student's junior year, they decide to major in elementary education and become a teacher, there is a good chance it will add four to five semesters before they can graduate. This is why I recommend a student take the core requirements for the first four semesters in college and mix in one or two of the courses they need for their major. Each university will have a listing of their core and major requirements. However, it is advantageous to declare a major because if a student is listed as "undeclared," their advisor may not be experienced in the area they finally declare. Undeclared major students are usually assigned to the School of Liberal Arts or other non-STEM programs, so it may be difficult for them to get into classes outside of the school where they are assigned. My recommendation is for an undecided student to declare Business as their major. They will receive a good overview of law, economics, and finance, which are solid foundations for any major.

It is important to understand the differences between departments and schools at a university. Most universities are organized by schools: like the School of Sciences, the School of Education, the School of Justice and Public Safety, the School of Building Science, the School of Arts, or some variation. Under each school are the various departments which could include the Department of Biology, which would typically be under the School of Sciences. The architecture department would be under the School of Building Science, and English would be under the School of Arts. Other Departments in the School of Sciences could be the Department of Mathematics or the Department of Chemistry, and every university is divided differently. Once a student knows what they want to study and the name of the major, they will be advised by a counselor or advisor under that specific School or Department. If you know you will do something in Education or the Sciences, try to pick a major under those schools so their paperwork won't be shuffled to another school when the student finally declares a major.

An example would be a pre-med student, usually a Biology/Chemistry major, who decides to change their major to English. Biology/Chemistry is traditionally housed in the School of Sciences, and English is usually found in the School of Arts. Some universities combine them into the School of Arts and Sciences. The university website will publish a listing of the Schools and Departments and what major is assigned under each of them.

Familiarize yourself with what majors are under what schools, deans, and department heads in each area in case a problem arises. Students should always start with the lowest level to address a problem. If a class is filled, contact the professor directly. Professors may have the authority to admit a student to a full class. If the professor can't help, contact the head of the department. The school's dean should be the last resort, but if the problem still isn't resolved, the Dean of Students or the Provost can also assist. A student needs to understand the hierarchy and the decision-makers in their major. It's also crucial for a student to understand not all courses in the same department may count toward their major.

Some schools/departments only accept specific courses. If the student is a Biology major and takes Biology for the non-major, the course may not transfer to the School of Sciences if the student seeks an undergraduate degree in Biology. Every college and university is different, so familiarize yourself with where your degree is housed, the requirements, and the department that administers the major and classes. Where do you find this information? The university should update its Student/Course Handbook every year. In the past, these were published in hardcopy and would be available to all students in lounges and throughout campus. However, now everything is online. Using the Student/ Course Handbook to determine your major requirements is very important. As handbooks are updated, so are the major requirements. If the Communicative Disorder major adds a class or renames a course after you start the program, you are generally grandfathered under the previous requirements. An example would be if the Communicative Disorder major adds a 3-hour course on Phonetics and Hearing, but you already took the Phonetics course a year prior as a freshman, which counted toward the degree. New students entering the program are now required to take the Phonetics and Hearing course. Since the student entered the program the previous year, their requirements for the major are under the previously published guidelines, which should be outlined in the Student/Course Handbook. This is where things get complicated, and advisors make mistakes. Ensure you follow the degree plan for the major based on the requirements published in the year you declared the major. It's a good idea to print/save the handbook from the year the student started the degree program.

Another issue is that the Departments and Schools at the same university compete for funding. The various Schools/ Department work well with each other but often it is an adversarial relationship because Schools and Departments compete for students. The more students, the more money the respective schools receive in their budget. For instance, a pre-law student could major in English, which could be under the School of Arts, or the student could major in pre-law, which might be under the Department of Criminal Justice in the School of Sciences. Both majors may help the student get into law school but the major and classes are under different schools with different requirements for graduation. Obviously, the English Department wants everyone to be an English major, just as the Department of Criminal Justice feels their major better prepares students for law school. Do your research. If most students accepted to a specific Law School are Criminal Justice majors or students accepted to a given Medical School are Chemistry majors instead of Biology majors, the student may want to select their field of study accordingly. On the other hand, some graduate schools do not require a specific undergraduate curriculum. One of the best law professors I know, who scored extremely high on the LSAT (Law School Aptitude Test) and graduated at the top of her class from Law School, was a Home Economics major. Some degrees, like Education and Nursing, require specific undergraduate courses for graduation. Graduate schools like Law and Medical School require a standardized test in addition to the undergraduate degree. Also, if the student doesn't have all the required courses for a particular graduate school, they may have to take "leveling classes" before or after admission, which can be expensive and time-consuming. Leveling classes are specific courses required for every student before admittance to some graduate schools, so research potential graduate schools and determine the basic requirements. In addition, some graduate schools do not accept grades below a "C" in specific courses. Do not waste money and time repeating a class or taking a leveling course. Do the research as an undergraduate student and take the required courses so they do not need to be repeated after graduation. The best way to ensure you do not need a leveling class is to check with the registrar of the graduate school. They will usually ask you to submit the syllabus and course description for the course, which would meet the requirements of the leveling class.

CHAPTER 14

CERTIFICATES

Universities award certificates in various areas like Leadership, Computer Programming, and Program Management. Some universities/colleges have separate certificate programs that don't require an associate or bachelor's degree. Depending on the certificate, there may not be an accreditation process associated with the certificate, which means any college can print out a certificate for taking a couple of classes. Is this a good idea? Once again, it depends. If a job requires a person to have a Cyber Security Certificate and the university provides this certificate for attending a three-hour seminar, it might be worth the effort. However, the certificate may not be worth the paper it is printed on and could cost a student thousands of dollars. Before you pay tuition or a fee to obtain a certificate, ask about the benefits of having the certificate, the requirements, and how it leads to a better-paying job. If the university can't answer those questions, then the certificate may have no value unless someone uses it for continuing education units (CEU). Some professional degrees, like architecture, speech pathology, and nursing, require yearly CEU. If this is the case, ensure the certificate lists the hours taken to obtain the certificate.

CHAPTER 15

GRADE ADJUSTMENT POLICIES, GRADE FORGIVENESS, ACADEMIC BANKRUPTCY

Now that you're in the college of your choice and enrolled in a program that leads to your major and, hopefully, a well-paying job, what happens if you receive a less-than-stellar grade? There are many reasons for a grade adjustment, but understanding how to obtain them and what they mean is essential so students can navigate the academic environment. Most new college students have a "period of adjustment;" they discover that obtaining an A in college is not as easy as in high school, especially if the course requires a good deal of independent study and reading. The old joke, "It's only reading if you do it," applies to many new college students.

Typically, new freshmen will get .5 lower than their high school grades their first semester unless they are engineering students, which can be an entire grade point lower. However, if a student or parent has "grade shock" when they see the first report card, there are several ways to raise the GPA, which varies by college.

Some colleges offer **grade forgiveness**. This is precisely what it implies. The university will "forgive" the grade, and in essence, it is removed from the transcript. Some universities allow up to four classes for grade forgiveness. There will be published guidelines (in the Student Handbook) on how to apply for grade forgiveness. Typically, the first step is for the student to fill out a form to have the grade removed, and sometimes, they must give a reason. Students can request grade forgiveness for any grade, but typically, it is done for grades of "D" or below. However, a student may want to use it for a "C" if their major won't accept a "C", and they will have to retake the course for graduate school. After the student requests grade forgiveness, their advisor or someone in the department must approve it, and the paperwork is sent to the registrar for removal. There may be an annotation on the transcript that the grade was removed or "forgiven." Students must follow up with the registrar to ensure the grade is removed or forgiven. Just because the paperwork was submitted doesn't mean the grade was removed from the transcript.

The apparent advantage of grade forgiveness is it allows a student to remove a failing grade from a course they may never retake or disliked without adversely impacting their GPA. It also allows a student to retake a course they failed and improve their GPA. Some colleges do not allow grade forgiveness for courses in their major or may only allow grade forgiveness once for the same course. I knew a student who used her grade forgiveness three times for Calculus and finally passed it on the fourth try, but it removed the previous "F" and "Ds" from her GPA. It also allows a student who may be placed on academic probation to raise their GPA and avoid probation.

A disadvantage of grade forgiveness is the student has to pay for the same course again. It may also encourage a student to "give up" on a course, especially if it's after the "drop date" for removing the class from your schedule—the student who took Calculus four times paid over $5000 for a 4-hour course. The colleges make additional money if a student asks for grade forgiveness because the student already paid for the class and the student may retake the same course. If the student is on scholarship or receiving Veterans Benefits for college, the benefits may not pay for the same course once a student receives a failing grade. The benefits will pay for the course if it is dropped before receiving a final grade. If tuition cost is a factor, a student may want to accept a "D" in the class. Although a "D" will lower a GPA, it is still a passing grade, and the student will receive the credit hours for taking the class.

Some universities don't offer grade forgiveness, but they may have another means for erasing a bad GPA, and it is called **academic bankruptcy.** This policy relates to a university negating an entire semester of course work and usually requires a reason like sickness, death of a family, member or another extenuating circumstance. This is common for students in their freshmen year who have trouble adjusting to college life or just discovered too many parties and didn't prioritize academics over their social life. This can be useful if a student has a disastrous semester. The entire semester's work and GPA will be removed, and if a student receives an "A" in one course, a "D" in another, and two "F"s, totaling four courses, all grades will be removed, and the student will have to repeat the entire semester but necessarily the same courses. The passing grades will also be removed, and the student must repeat those courses. This is an extreme measure, but I would argue it's better the keeping it on their GPA. It's almost impossible to recover from a GPA below 1.0, and it's better to remove and repeat the entire semester than spend four years trying to recover from one bad semester.

Another grade adjustment policy includes an "I" for incomplete. Professors can allow a student to complete the course after the end of the semester, and most colleges allow up to a year to complete the coursework. Sometimes, an "I" is used if a military student is called to active duty and may deploy and be unable to attend class or complete the course requirements. Students may receive an "I" if they become ill and cannot complete the class. There are numerous reasons for a student to request an "I" for a grade, and an "I" is better than dropping the class due to cost; the course doesn't have to be retaken because the student will eventually receive a grade and credit. The professor will work with the student and develop a plan to complete the coursework. Each plan is different and depends on the student and professor. The "I" will remain on the transcript for a year, and if the student does not complete the work, the "I" will change to an "F," so if the professor inputs an "I" for the grade and allows the student to complete the work later, ensure the grade is updated once the course work is complete.

If a student drops the course, a code of "W" for withdrawal will be annotated on the transcript. Another code on a transcript is "FA," which means failure to attend and pertains to students who sign up and pay for a course but do not attend, usually within the first ten days of the class. Since financial aid, grants, scholarships, and VA benefits are tied to attendance, most universities verify attendance within the first two weeks of class. This is usually done with a syllabus exam, asking students basic questions about what was on the syllabus. If a student doesn't respond or show up for class, the professor will submit an attendance report to the registrar's office, and the student will be dropped, and an "FA" will appear on the transcript. Everyone makes mistakes and realize a professor is also capable of making a mistake with grades and reports, especially in a classroom with over 100 students. If this happens, the professor will submit a "grade adjustment" request automatically or after it is brought to their attention.

At most universities, professors are given a date to submit final grades. Obviously, if a student is a graduating senior, those grades are given priority since the registrar must post them before graduation t0 ensure the student meets the requirements for graduation. Professors may be hesitant to submit a grade change after final grades are submitted because, quite honestly, it requires work and usually the signature of the department head and dean of the school. If a professor makes an error in grade computation, the mistake would be highlighted to their supervisor, who may keep track of grade changes. Professors make mistakes all the time, and no one should get mad if a student challenges a grade or draws attention to a computation error. However, some professors consider it a personal attack when a student appeals a grade for a specific assignment or an entire class. An issue pertaining to grades and grades on assignments should be brought to the professor's attention. However, if a student still feels the problem was not appropriately addressed, the Student Handbook will provide a process for adjudication. I advise students to review the Faculty

Handbook because rules and regulations regarding grades also govern faculty and how to address violations of academic integrity. Plagiarism, looking up answers on the phone during an exam, and other forms of cheating all violate academic integrity. How a professor deals with violations may vary by instructor, but the best advice is not to commit offenses in the first place; then, the students won't have to defend themselves against it. Yet, there may be a question on an assignment or grade that needs to be addressed, and if both the student and the professor feel they are correct, I recommend that the student begin with a review of the course syllabus.

A good syllabus addresses the course objectives, due dates for assignments, scoring for exams and course work, how to contact the instructor, course expectations, and procedures for missing classes or assignments, and it should also address matters pertaining to academic dishonesty. The first step for any grade adjustment is to consult the instructor's syllabus. For example, if the syllabus states the midterm is 50% of the class grade, and the final is the other 50% of the grade, but the syllabus does not address class attendance or quizzes and the student receives "A"s on both the midterm and the final, the grade should be an "A" in the course. However, the instructor lowered the grade to a "B" because the student never attended class. The student would have a valid case for appealing the grade and requesting a grade adjustment. A good syllabus will assign points for each assignment and include a rubric for how the assignment will be graded or scored. Suppose the professor uses a Learning Management System (LMS) like CANVAS or BlackBoard and inputs the grades/points into the LMS. In that case, the scoring for the final grade could be incorrect if the points are not appropriately weighted in the LMS or the professor hits the wrong number or grade when inputting data. I always asked my students to review their grades before I submitted them to the registrar. Yes, a grade adjustment can be made after the final grade is reported, but the process is more difficult, and most colleges want a justification for the grade change.

If the matter is still not resolved to the student's satisfaction, there should be procedures for appeal outlined in the Student Handbook. These usually involve elevating the issue to the head of the department and finally to the dean. Students should always try to resolve problems promptly and not wait until the end of the course to dispute a grade on a quiz given on the first day of the class. Also, everyone makes mistakes, and approaching the professor with a bad attitude or beginning the conversation with, "You were wrong and messed up my grade," does not facilitate a collegial discussion. Students should show respect if they expect to receive respect. A student is an adult in college and expected to act in a manner commensurate with their standing. I am much more receptive to listening to students who exemplify a positive attitude and respect others. Also, if the professor doesn't know your name, don't be offended; larger classes and numerous sessions make it difficult to remember everyone.

If a student is trying to address an issue and uses email, the subject line should state the name of the class, the session, the time the class meets, and the problem. An example would be, Biology 112, 8:00 am, Wednesday and Friday, request grade review. State the bottom line up front in the first paragraph with a purpose statement. Example: The purpose of this email is to request a review of my grade on Quiz 1, question 2, and my final grade on the exam. I included the answer to the question, but my response was marked incorrect, and this lowered my grade from 95% to 90%. The student should screen capture and attach the disputed grade/question and make an appointment to discuss the matter personally if it can't be resolved via email or other method. Most professors are not offended if a student highlights a grading error. Personally, if most of my students get a question wrong on an exam, I sometimes exclude the question from grading.

A student's final grade is their responsibility. If a professor makes a mistake and the student doesn't attempt to correct it before the next semester begins, some colleges will not grant a grade change or adjustment. Review the timeliness for redress of a grade or any matter requiring an academic review. In addition, some universities do not remove a failing grade or low grade if a student retakes the same course and receives a passing grade. If you fail Calculus and retake it the next semester and receive an "A," the university will average the two grades for a 2.0 or a "C," so understand the rules before retaking a class. If this is the case, dropping the course before you fail is more advantageous because of the negative repercussions on your GPA.

Finally, just like an actor must know their audience, a student should know their professor. Originally, I wasn't going to include this in the book, but I've had so many parents and students complain about this issue, I wanted to make prospective students and parents aware of it. Some professors are brilliant but can't teach, and others can't separate their personal opinions from academic responsibilities. My son had a paper with the comments, "Too well researched, and you supported your thesis well, but I disagree with your comment about no taxation without representation." My son used the US Constitution as a reference and tax law and codes to support his argument, but it was counter to what the teacher believed, so she lowered his grade. Although this may not be the norm, students should be aware of this issue. Also, some professors see themselves as "gatekeepers," and because their course might be perceived as an easy "A," they make it more difficult than it needs, and they brag that very few of their students get an "A" in the class. If you are a great instructor, most of your students will receive a "B" or an "A." I would also caution against taking a class from a professor who's never worked in the field as a practitioner and spent all their time in college. I also joked about taking a business class from someone who never actually ran a business or an economist who didn't know when the country was in a recession.

Ask other students who took the same class what they thought or if the professor had any pet peeves or other class nuances before you sign up for their class. Sometimes, a particular professor may be their only choice for a required class, but if there is a choice, select the professor who better aligns with your learning style and maybe even politics. Although politics should be kept out of the classroom, faculty have become much more liberal, and their political views could bleed into their teaching.

True Story: *A friend's daughter had a mandatory women's study class with a liberal professor. The student said to pass the class, she had to agree with everything the teacher said. The student wrote her assignments from a liberal perspective. She told her father she disagreed with the professor on most subjects, but if she didn't write her papers from a liberal* *perspective, she would receive a lower grade. The student said the professor was very hostile to males and conservatives in the class and gave them lower grades, even if they supported their papers with facts and cited references. One assignment consisted of attending a "Me Too" or "Black Lives Matter" (BLM) rally, and a student wasn't comfortable attending either of these groups. The professor gave him a failing grade on the assignment because he refused to participate in the rally.*

The student may want to parrot what the professor says in class and on exams to avoid a grade dispute or receiving a lower grade on an assignment, even if the student disagrees with the instructor or can provide academic sources where the course material is incorrect. Of course, the same could apply to a conservative professor and a liberal student. Regardless, know your audience.

There's a saying in academia, "Do the research you have to do to get your PhD, then do the research you want to do once you have it." I would argue this is good advice for students who want to finish college. Do what you need to do to graduate, then do what you want to do once you have the degree. No one should compromise their integrity, but there are times to pick your battle, and arguing with a professor on a particular issue may not be the time or the place.

FINAL THOUGHTS

I wish I could go back in time to my undergraduate days with what I've learned after working over twenty years in higher education; the first thing I would do is **attend every class and be on time, dressed professionally.** Students who show up for class every session rarely fail, and in my personal experience, they usually receive a "B" or higher. If you are not an early riser, don't take the 8:00 am class. There is a reason that session is rarely closed and has open seats. I made this mistake as an undergraduate, and a review of my Chemistry grade would verify I didn't attend most of the time, and when I did, I was in sweatpants and sometimes a clean shirt. I would have flunked me just for how I dressed in class.

Don't buy the books until the first day of class and only after verifying from the syllabus that you'll use them. College bookstores are there to make a profit. Once you sign up for a class, the bookstore will list the resources required for the class. I spent thousands of dollars on books I never opened because the bookstore said I needed them for a class. Some professors write their own books. These tend to be expensive because they may self-publish and are difficult to resell. Most of the time, Amazon or another book retailer will sell the same book at a reduced price but verify the ISBN.

Students with scholarships that include books may have to purchase the books from the bookstore to be reimbursed or have the cost of the books paid by the scholarship.

If you have to work, get a job that complements your degree or allows you to study. I was a lifeguard, so if no one was swimming, I could study, although I spent more time worrying about what I was wearing to the football game and afterparty. If you are studying architecture, try to find a position in an architecture firm. If you're in the medical field, you can never have too many observation or clinical hours. When you graduate, you'll have experience in your field, a resume builder, and a possible point of contact for a good position in your field of study, which should be the ultimate goal after graduation.

Enroll in business, accounting, and finance classes. Most degrees allow for a small number of electives, which are courses that may not be in the student's major field of study but count toward total credit hours for graduation. I would tell my students you don't need college to make money but you need college to keep the money you make. As an undergraduate student, I studied Biology and Psychology. As an adult, I started my own contracting company, and while I understood how the human body and brain functioned, I wish I had majored in business and finance. Everyone must pay taxes, and I was surprised at how little I knew about the real world after I graduated. I had to navigate payroll, taxes, investments, and finance. Some universities require students to minor in another subject, which could be an excellent opportunity to take courses on life skills. If the university requires a physical education course, take something fun like tennis, golfing, or swimming and explore open elective courses. My son took kayaking, and my daughter enrolled in SCUBA diving.

Use the college placement programs, resume writing resources, and alumni office. Universities track students after graduation and want to see you succeed because they hope you'll become recruiters and active alumni who will hopefully donate to the university. Attend the job fairs before graduation and make contacts with future employers. Interview for a job even if you don't want the position because it's good practice for the position you may want later. If you give an employer a resume or have an interview within 24 hours, send a follow-up email or call.

Talk to your professors and instructors. I never failed a student I knew was trying and attended every class and set up an appointment to review course material if they were struggling. Some colleges have programs like "Take a Professor to Lunch," and the university will pay the bill for a professor and student to do lunch or dinner in the student union. Professors were once students, and not all professors were "A" students, so they understand if you have a problem in a class. Let them help you, but you must ask for help before it's too late to save the grade.

Use the free tutoring services offered at most colleges. Universities have "student success" offices or something similar and provide tutoring services. Find a study group or form one. Apps like GroupMe, TEAMs, and Zoom can also provide a resource for students to work in groups and study together. If you are having trouble in a class, I guarantee someone else is also. You wouldn't just sit behind your desk if you have a problem at work. You would ask for help and find out "what right looks like" so you don't flounder and drown. Colleges are expensive, and they don't want to see you fail because it impacts their graduation and retention rates, which could affect the university's accreditation.

Save money! Find scholarship money or be a Residential Assistant (RA). There are scholarships for almost anything; you need to find one and do the paperwork. If you're left-handed, there is a scholarship. If your parents were in a sorority or fraternity, there is a scholarship. Even a $100 scholarship will pay for a book. Yes, everyone wants the full-ride scholarship for all tuition and books, but there are other smaller scholarships, and if you get enough of the smaller scholarships, they add up and can equal one more extensive scholarship. Although not available for freshmen, RAs usually receive free room and board and may get paid. If you are living in the dorm anyway, you can earn money for supervising other students. Apply early for these positions because they are competitive.

Establish set hours for studying and use the library. Some students can study an hour before an exam and pass it. However, the other 99% have to study and prepare for exams. Students who have a set schedule and find a quiet place without distractions are more likely to succeed. Leaving your apartment or dorm requires more effort, but just finding a new location and going there every day establishes a routine, which turns into a habit and can provide positive results. It's also an excellent opportunity to meet other people in your class who want to study.

Exercise and practice good nutrition. A healthy body and mind are conducive to learning. Also, exercise relieves stress, and college is stressful. It's incredible what a two-mile run or 30-minute walk can do to focus your brain. Walking to class doesn't count as exercise unless your brain is uncluttered on the walk and you're running an

8-minute mile to class. Find time at least 3- 5 times a week to do some cardio activity for 30 minutes or more. Some colleges have sports clubs and intermural sports, so if you like team sports, it should be easy to find something you enjoy. Eating well can be more of a challenge because fast food is everywhere, convenient, easy, and sometimes less expensive. Most students gain weight during their freshmen year. It's sometimes referred to as the "Freshmen 15," but it could also be a time to get in shape. The best advice to avoid this is simple: avoid pizza and fried foods, eat fresh fruit and vegetables, and avoid free beer at parties.

Have fun…but not too much. College is much more than going to class and studying. There's a scene in the movie *Back to School* where Rodney Dangerfield plays a successful businessman who goes back to college to prove to his son he can do it, and he is selected to give the graduation commencement speech. He says, "Don't go! It's a Jungle out there! Stay in School!" I would agree, and recently my daughter told me she "hates adulting" and misses college. It can be a wonderful experience where you meet lifelong friends and prepare for a rewarding career. It can also be horrendous and a complete waste of time and money. Like everything in life, it's about the choices you make. It always broke my heart to see a student with so much potential fail or drop out because they partied more than they studied or didn't use the resources available to help them succeed. It's cliché, but the only time someone fails is when they stop trying. Don't be that person.